César Chá

The Farm Worker's Friend

Maria Fleming

Rigby

A Harcourt Achieve Imprint

www.Rigby.com
1-800-531-5015

From the time he was a boy, César Chávez worked in the fields of California. He picked fruits and vegetables. It was hot, dirty work.

César and the rest of his family spent many hours bending over crops. They filled box after box with ripe tomatoes, berries, and peas. They worked hard all day.

Like many other Mexican Americans, César and his
family were **migrant** farm workers. They moved from
town to town. They picked crops in the fields.

Although they worked all day long until night time, farm workers didn't make a lot of money. This was unfair. Sometimes César's family did not have enough food to eat or a house to live in.

César never went to high school because his family moved around a lot. The family needed the money that César made working in the fields.

When César was older, he worked in the **vineyards** in California. He learned how to take care of grapes and pick them. He was good at it.

César thought that farm workers should make more money for the hard work they did. He also thought that the farm owners should treat workers better.

César formed a group called a **union.** This group would ask the farm owners to treat them fairly. If all the farm workers asked for the same things, César believed that the farm owners would have to listen to them. Then the farm owners would give the workers what they needed.

César talked to many farm workers. He went from town to town asking them to be in his union. He told the group that if they worked together, they could make their lives better.

Many women and men became part of the new group of farm workers. They were happy that César was helping them.

Some union workers decided to stop working until they got more money for picking grapes. This is called a **strike.** They would not go back to work until they got what they wanted.

The vineyard owners still did not give the workers more money. That was unfair.

By this time, people across the country had heard about the strike in the vineyards. They agreed with the workers. They sent food, clothing, and money to help them.

César thought people could help the workers in another way, too. He asked people not to buy grapes.

People listened to César! They stopped buying grapes. This hurt the vineyard owners. When fewer people bought their grapes, the owners made less money.

Finally the vineyard owners agreed to pay the workers more money. The workers agreed to go back to work. The workers had won! They were very happy!

Because so many other farm workers were treated unfairly, César spent the rest of his life working to help them.

César Chávez was a hero who tried to make our country a better place.

César Chávez Time Line

Chávez is born March 21 near Yuma, Arizona.

He works for the rights of Mexican Americans.

Members strike after vineyard owners refuse to give better pay.

1927   **1937**   **1952**   **1962** **1965**

The Chávez family members become migrant farm workers.

He forms a union.

The five-year strike is successful and comes to an end.

Chavez dies April 23 in San Luis, Arizona.

1967 **1970** **1979** **1993** **1994**

People agree not to buy grapes.

The union strikes against other vegetable growers for better pay.

He receives the Presidential Medal of Freedom.

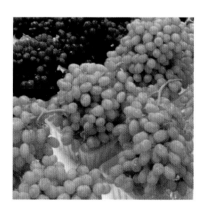

Glossary

migrant   person who moves from town to town
to find work

strike   to stop a work activity for a good reason

union   group of people who join together
for a special reason

vineyards   farms where grapes are planted